The Future of Life on Earth

Michael Bright

www.raintreepublishers.co.uk
Visit our website to find out more information about Raintree books.

To order:
☎ Phone 0845 6044371
🖨 Fax +44 (0) 1865 312263
📧 Email myorders@raintreepublishers.co.uk

Customers from outside the UK please telephone +44 1865 312262

Raintree is an imprint of Capstone Global Library Limited, a company incorporated in England and Wales having its registered office at 7 Pilgrim Street, London, EC4V 6LB – Registered company number: 6695582

Text © Capstone Global Library Limited 2012
First published in hardback in 2012
Paperback edition first published in 2013
The moral rights of the proprietor have been asserted.

Edited by Andrew Farrow, Adrian Vigliano, and Diyan Leake
Designed by Victoria Allen
Picture research by Elizabeth Alexander
Original illustrations © Capstone Global Library Ltd 2012
Illustrations by Oxford Designers & Illustrators
Originated by Capstone Global Library Ltd
Printed in China

ISBN 978 1 406 23255 4 (hardback)
15 14 13 12 11
10 9 8 7 6 5 4 3 2 1

ISBN 978 1 406 23262 2 (paperback)
16 15 14 13 12
10 9 8 7 6 5 4 3 2 1

British Library Cataloguing in Publication Data
Bright, Michael.
The future of life on Earth. -- (The web of life)
576-dc22
A full catalogue record for this book is available from the British Library.

Acknowledgements
The author and publisher are grateful to the following for permission to reproduce copyright material: Alamy pp. 27 (© Papilio), 35 (© The Art Archive); Cédric d'Udekem d'Acoz, RBINS, 2007 p. 8 top; Census of Marine Life, E. Paul Oberlander, Woods Hole Oceanographic Institution p. 7; Getty Images p. 26 (Joel Sartore); Laurence Madin/ Woods Hole Oceanographic Institution p. 8 bottom; NASA p. 41 (JPL/University of Arizona); (JPL-Caltech) p. 36; Photolibrary pp. 4 (J-L. Klein & M-L. Hubert), 5 (Brandon Cole), 15 (Corbis), 16 (Denis Meyer), 18 (WU HONG/epa), 19 (Brandon Cole), 20 (S.J. Krasemann), 21 (Martin Page), 22 (Jeff Vanuga), 24 (Oxford Scientific), 29 (RAF MAKDA), 31 (DesignPics Inc.), 32 (Gerard Soury), 37 (Detlev van Ravenswaay), 39 (Franco Banfi), 40 (Detlef van Ravenswaay); Science Photo Library pp. 11 (Shaun Baesman / US Geological Survey), 38 (Walter Myers); Shutterstock pp. 10 (© janr34), 12 (© JeremyRichards), 17 (© Durden Images), 25 (© Monkey Business Images); Tin-Yam Chan, National Taiwan Ocean University, Keelung p.9; Zoological Society of San Diego p. 28.

Cover photograph of a Royal Bengal tiger taking a bath at an algae pond reproduced with permission of Shutterstock (© neelsky).

Every effort has been made to contact copyright holders of material reproduced in this book. Any omissions will be rectified in subsequent printings if notice is given to the publisher.

Contents

Some words appear in the text in bold, **like this**. You can find out what they mean by looking in the glossary.

Biodiversity

Did you know that there may be as many as 500 million **species** of living things on Earth? This great variety of life represents the **biodiversity** of the planet.

Most of the larger animals have been fairly well categorized. However, many of the smaller living things on this planet have yet to be discovered, let alone described. Nobody actually knows the true total.

Biodiversity hot spots

Biodiversity is not the same all over the world. Tropical countries have far more species than polar regions. Tropical rainforests, for example, cover just 6 per cent of Earth's surface, yet they contain 50 per cent of the world's plants and animals. Forests in **temperate** Europe and North America average 20 species of tree per **hectare**, while a single national park in the tropics – Manu National Park in Peru – has more than 220 species per hectare.

Tropical rainforests are thought to be the richest wildlife areas on the planet. They are home to animals such as this jaguar.

Biodiversity and keystone species

Biodiversity is important because every species is dependent on others, especially for food. Plant-eaters need plants, **predators** need **prey**, and **parasites** need hosts. In any **ecosystem**, there are certain species called keystone species that seem to be especially important for maintaining biodiversity. If a keystone species is removed, the balance of nature can be upset.

Biodiversity threatened

Today, biodiversity is suffering a setback because humans are destroying the **habitats** of plants and animals, upsetting the climate, and polluting the **environment**. Between 5 and 10 per cent of species are thought to become extinct each decade due to tropical rainforest destruction alone.

Sea urchins are frequently the prey of sea otters.

What is a keystone species?

A keystone species is one that has a significant impact on an ecosystem, even though its size and numbers seem small. If it disappears, there may be two knock-on effects:

1. Other species that depend on it will become extinct, too, forming "chains of extinction".

2. The species that it normally eats increases in numbers.

The sea otter of North America's Pacific coast is a keystone species. It eats sea urchins, among other things. In areas where the otter is extinct, sea urchin numbers increase. Sea urchins eat kelp (a type of seaweed), so the kelp disappears. With it goes an enormous number of species that depend on kelp for food and living space. The seabed is overrun by sea urchins, and an entire marine ecosystem is destroyed.

CASE STUDY

Census of Marine Life

Are there monsters in the sea? If there are, the Census of Marine Life (COML) is likely to find them. COML is a project involving marine scientists from 80 nations who are trying to answer these questions:

- What kinds of life inhabit the oceans?

- What lives where?

- How many individuals of each species lives there, and how many are likely to be there in the future?

To find the answers to these big questions, scientists having been using the very latest equipment to sample life in the oceans.

1 Scientists explore above and below the pack ice in polar seas.

2 Aircraft sense animals under the surface using the scattering of light.

3 Animals carry tags recording their activity, linked to satellites in space.

4 **Echolocation** equipment tracks fish travelling up and down.

5 Camera platforms record life on the deep-sea floor.

6 Submersibles take scientists deep down to see animals living in the deep sea.

7 Unmanned submersibles go where people cannot.

8 Nets and dredges catch specimens at all depths for closer study.

COML: the first 10 years

COML began in 2000 and its first report was published in 2010. Over 2,700 scientists embarked on 540 expeditions across all the world's oceans. They created the first comprehensive list of known species – passing 190,000 in September 2010 – and discovered 6,000 new species. In fact, everywhere the scientists looked they found life – in places hot enough to melt lead, in ice, and in places where there is barely any light and oxygen.

WHAT IT MEANS FOR US

The COML is still unable to assess how many species live in the sea. There is more than 20 per cent of the ocean for which there is no data at all. However, habitat destruction, overfishing, and rising water temperatures – all caused by humans – are taking their toll, even in the deepest parts of the ocean. It means that we could be exterminating species before we even know of their existence.

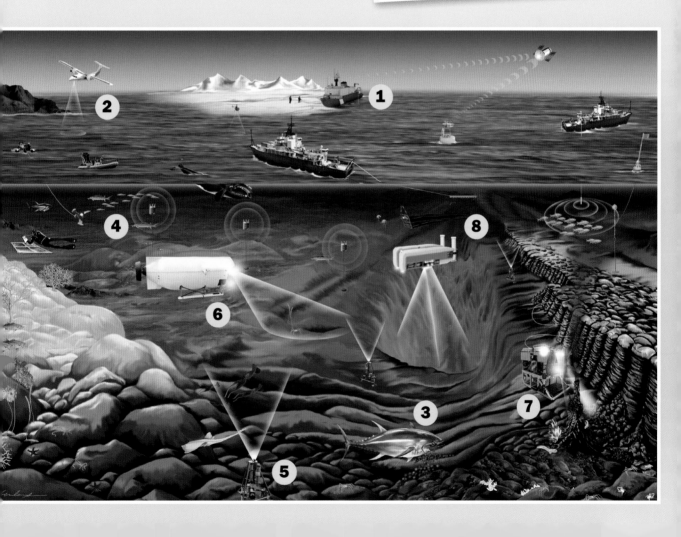

New species

Here are just a few of the 6,000 new species that COML expeditions discovered in different parts of the world.

During International Polar Year (2007–2008), COML surveyed an area of icy waters 10,000 kilometres square (4,000 miles square) and 850 metres (half a mile) deep. They found many new species of sea life, including this *Lysianassoid*, in the seabed off Antarctica.

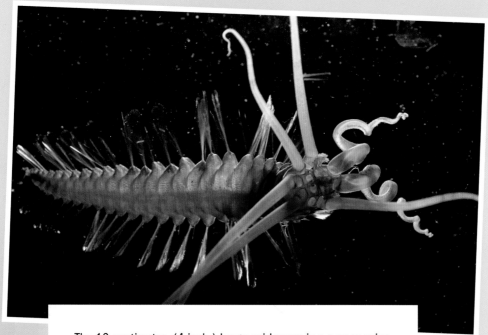

The 10 centimetre- (4 inch-) long squid worm is a new species of **annelid worm**. It was discovered in water 2,800 metres (9,000 metres) deep in the Celebes Sea. It was discovered by scientists from the Woods Hole Oceanographic Institution, adding another new species to COML.

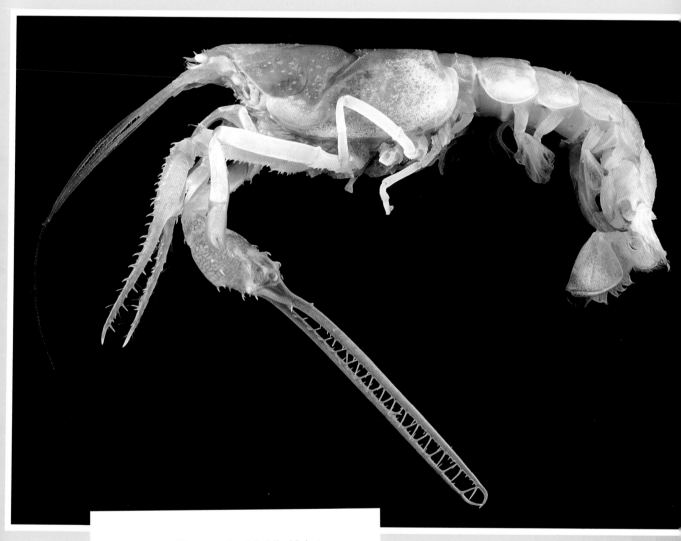

The scientific name for this blind lobster
is *Dinochelus ausubeli,* from the Greek for
"terrible and fearful claw" and in honour of
Jesse Ausubel, a co-founder of COML.

Winners and losers

Global **biodiversity** is decreasing – that's a fact. The reason is that humans today are having a huge impact on life on Earth. The increasing human population, **habitat** destruction, overfishing, overhunting, widespread pollution, and human-induced **climate change** are changing the **environment** and pushing many **species** to the brink of extinction. However, some species have **adapted** to our excesses and wastes, and they are thriving.

Generalists and specialists

Plants and animals can be divided into "generalists" and "specialists". The generalists are able to adapt rapidly to changing conditions. They can live virtually anywhere. They tend to be the winners when conditions change quickly.

The specialists have **evolved** to live in a particular place with particular conditions. If there is a major change in their environment, they have a limited ability to adapt and could well die out. Specialists can more easily become losers. One of these two groups often lives close to humans. Which do you think it might be?

WHAT IT MEANS FOR US

Some animals, such as rats, cockroaches, red foxes, and racoons, are born survivors. They are generalists. They have adapted to living with us by feeding on our rubbish, or invading our homes and gardens. Magpies, crows, gulls, ants, and weeds such as dandelions are other examples of generalists that adapt to most environments.

In North America, racoons enter towns and raid dustbins and even live in people's houses.

On the edge of what's possible

It was always thought that cockroaches could survive a nuclear explosion, but we now know they can be killed by **radiation** just like us. However, there are a handful of **organisms** known as extremophiles that can survive in extreme conditions. One of these is an organism that survives high levels of radiation, as well as surviving in a **vacuum**, or in extreme cold or heat.

Scientists have also discovered an extremophile in the warm pools at Mono Lake in California. This **bacterium** manufactures food for itself by using arsenic, a chemical that will kill most other organisms. It all means that no matter how much we alter the environment now and in the future, there are likely to be life forms that will adapt and live in it.

These organisms from Mono Lake make use of the deadly poison arsenic.

Population pressure

Some scientists believe that one of the biggest threats to the future of life on Earth is the number of people living here. In 2010, the world population was nearly 7 billion. According to United Nations (UN) forecasts, this number will rise to 9.22 billion by 2075. All these people need a place to live, fresh water to drink, clean air to breathe, and land to grow food.

The natural world is cracking under the pressure of so many people. And if Nature suffers, people suffer, too.

- According to the UN World Health Organization, unclean water and poor sanitation currently kills over 12 million people each year. Air pollution kills 3 million people.

- The UN Food and Agricultural Organization indicates that in 64 out of 105 developing countries, the population is growing faster than food supplies.

By 2100, there will be 2,000 people per square kilometre (800 people per square mile) in Bangladesh.

Can science help?

So, how might developments in science, medicine, and agriculture affect the global population? The incidence of major killer diseases and hunger could decrease. Agricultural developments, such as **genetically modified** crops, might enable poor farmers to grow food where it was difficult before. **Desalination** plants, which remove salt from seawater, and **rain-seeding** of clouds might bring water to hot, dry regions. The result could be an increase in how long people live.

The graph below shows the world population from 1800 to the present, and UN estimates up to 2100. Depending on the country, **life expectancy** rises could be from 66–97 years in 2100 to 87–106 years in 2300. This means a further burden on the **environment**.

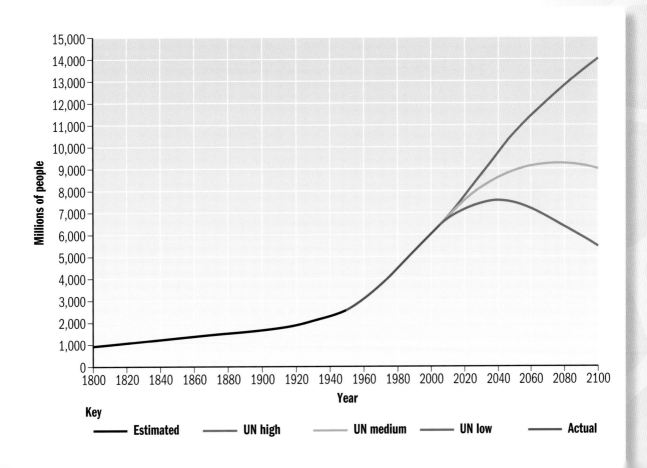

Key

Estimated   UN high   UN medium   UN low   Actual

A change in the weather

Earth's climate is changing – and that's a fact. It is getting warmer. The past decade, from January 2000 to December 2009, was the warmest on record. However, the reasons for the change are the subject of an international debate.

The impact of humans

Most scientists believe that humans are the cause. We generate vast quantities of **greenhouse gases**, such as carbon dioxide (CO_2). This is produced when we burn carbon-based (fossil) fuels, such as oil, natural gas, and coal, in vehicles, factories, and power stations. When CO_2 reaches the atmosphere, it absorbs heat and radiates it back into the lower atmosphere. This makes the air temperature higher than if the heat came directly from the Sun alone. The result is global warming.

A few scientists think that the present **climate change** is due to natural, long-term cycles such as the amount of heat we receive from the Sun.

This graph shows the average global temperature from 1880 to 2010. The temperature during the past decade was 0.8°C (1.44°F) warmer than at start of the 20th century, with two-thirds of the warming occurring since 1975.

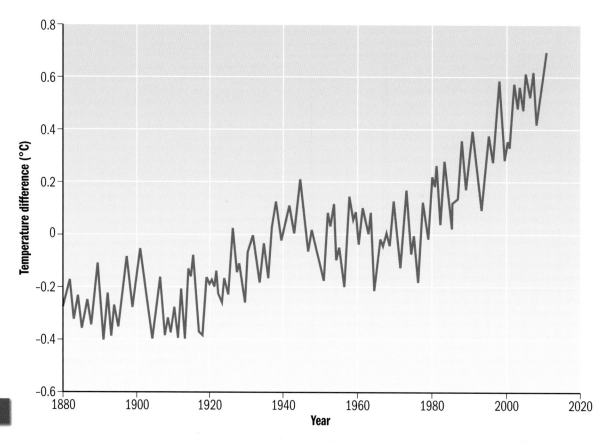

Climate refugees

The first human victims of climate change are likely to be the inhabitants of small islands such as those in the Pacific Ocean. Higher global temperatures cause polar ice to melt, resulting in a rise in sea level. The warming ocean also expands, adding to the problem.

Currently, global sea level rise is 2.8–3.1 millimetres ($^{11}/_{100}$–$^{12}/_{100}$ inch) per year. Eventually the sea will cover the islands completely. Wildlife species will disappear, and the human inhabitants will be forced to leave their homes.

Common confusions

Ozone and global warming

Shrinking of Earth's ozone layer in the lower part of the **stratosphere** is not a direct cause of global warming, although there are some links. It is caused by gases called chlorofluorocarbons (CFCs) from **aerosol** cans, rather than by CO_2. It results in more harmful levels of **ultraviolet radiation** reaching Earth's surface, which is damaging to life. It can cause skin cancer in humans.

Habitats on the coast of the Bay of Bengal are home to Bengal tigers. Studies have shown that sea levels are rising at such a rate that most of the tigers' territory will be under water by 2070.

Climate casualties

Islands in the Bay of Bengal became one of the first victims of climate change and the rise in sea level. Lohachara Island disappeared below the waves in 1996, forcing its human inhabitants to live on the mainland. In 2009, New Moore Island (also known as South Talpatti) was drowned by the sea.

WORD BANK
greenhouse gas   gas that absorbs the Sun's energy and radiates it back into the atmosphere

Water, water everywhere

Fresh water is essential for life. With over 70 per cent of the planet's surface covered by water, globally there is no water shortage. The problem is that the water is not in the right place or it is badly managed, or it is salt water. Ninety-seven per cent of Earth's water is in the oceans, and 1 per cent is locked up as ice. Little more than one-hundredth of 1 per cent of the world's water is in lakes, rivers, and shallow **groundwater**, and available for people and wildlife to use.

WHAT IT MEANS FOR US

Water is not only needed for drinking. It is also important for agriculture, industry, and in our towns and cities. Water shortages have an impact on world food supply and on our health. The more people there are, the greater the demand for water. Freshwater usage worldwide tripled during the 20th century, and is currently doubling every 21 years. If this trend continues, it is estimated that by 2025 severe water shortages will affect one-third of all the people on Earth.

Some people only have access to polluted water. Clean water is vital for food and health. Scarcity of water can cause political unrest and even wars.

Outback nomads

Many wildlife communities need fresh water in order to survive. For example, in Australia's **outback**, huge numbers of water birds depend on water that appears only occasionally.

Lake Eyre is a hot, dry **saltpan** where rain rarely falls. However, just once or twice in a decade, water that fell as rain thousands of kilometres away in the tropical north of Australia flows across the desert and into Lake Eyre. The eggs of tiny creatures, such as brine shrimps, which have lain **dormant** in the salt for years, suddenly hatch out.

Fish, swept in by the temporary feeder rivers, eat the shrimps. Tens of thousands of water birds arrive from all over Australia and beyond to catch the fish. They breed there in the middle of the desert while there is this sudden glut of food. How all the birds know when to come is a mystery, but their presence or their absence in the outback is a good indication of the health of Australia's inland waterways.

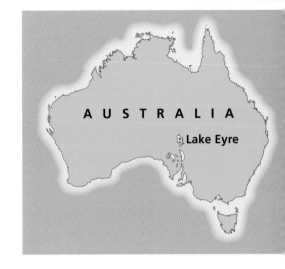

Tens of thousands of Australian pelicans leave the coastal areas and head to the desert to breed when Lake Eyre (see map above) floods once or twice in a decade.

Contaminated world

Pollution can come from many sources: chemicals, noise, heat, and light. Whatever the source, it **contaminates** the natural **environment** and can harm living things, including humans.

Linfen in China is thought to be the most polluted place on the planet.

Across frontiers

Pollution produced in one part of the world can end up in another part, even thousands of kilometres away. For example, pollution created in Europe, Russia, and North America drifts into the Arctic. It then enters the food chain. Tiny **organisms** in the oceans pick up the contaminants. Small fish eat the organisms. The small fish are, in turn, eaten by larger fish – and so on up the chain to seals, polar bears, and killer whales. At each stage in the chain, the contaminants are **concentrated**. Eventually, the animals at the top of the chain are storing so many poisonous chemicals in their bodies, they could be labelled "Danger: **Toxic** Waste Dump".

The table below reveals the top five toxic threats during 2010.

Toxic pollutant	Population at risk at identified polluted sites	Global impact
1. Lead	10.0 million	18–22 million
2. Mercury	8.6 million	15–19 million
3. Chromium	7.3 million	13–17 million
4. Arsenic	3.7 million	5–9 million
5. Pesticides	3.4 million	5–8 million

Questions to think about

Can you suggest other top **predators** that might have concentrated toxic chemicals in their bodies? Could some of the foods we eat be contaminated with pollutants?

According to the Norwegian Polar Institute, killer whales have overtaken polar bears as the most contaminated animals in the Arctic.

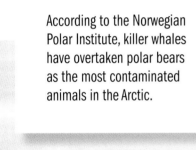

WHAT IT MEANS FOR US

We like to eat fish for the healthy oils they contain. However, some fish may contain high levels of pollutants, too. The skipjack tuna picks up so many contaminants that scientists use it as a "bioindicator" **species**. They found dangerous **pesticides** and industrial chemicals that have been banned by developed nations since the 1970s. In the North Atlantic, close to the developed nations, levels of these chemicals in the tuna fish are dropping. However, in the central Pacific Ocean, close to nations that still use these polluting chemicals, levels are rising.

In the wrong place at the wrong time

Alien or invasive **species** are plants or animals that have been removed from their normal **habitat**. They are then released, either deliberately or accidentally, into a new place. They can disrupt the natural **ecosystems** in their new homes to such an extent that they are believed to be responsible for a serious loss of **biodiversity** across the globe.

Without the plants and animals with which they normally interact, especially **predators** and **parasites**, invasive species multiply and become serious pests. They sometimes do so well that they push out or kill resident species.

Alien ants

One of the world's most successful alien invaders is the Argentinean fire ant. It normally lives in South America, but it is now a pest in the United States, Australia, Taiwan, the Philippines, China, and southern Europe. It arrived by hitching a ride with goods on board ships.

In Europe, fire ants have created truly gigantic "supercolonies", where ants move freely between a vast network of nests. The largest supercolony is on a strip of land stretching along the Mediterranean coast from Italy to Spain. This free flow of ants between nests is thought to be the main reason why the ants can take over areas so successfully.

Fire ants are found far from their normal home in Argentina.

WHAT IT MEANS FOR US

Fire ants travel about in agricultural products such as grass turf for garden lawns, and they set up new nests overnight. They kill birds and newborn calves and their stings are painful to humans. Some people have even died from fire ant stings. The ants are predators of agricultural pests and this has benefits for farmers. However, they come at a cost. The ants also kill native ground-nesting bees and other natural **pollinators** of crops. In the United States, $5 billion (£3.10 billion) is spent on medical treatment and $750 million (£465 million) on agricultural damage caused by fire ants each year.

Pretty but deadly

Japanese knotweed (below) was introduced into Europe and North America in the 19th century as an ornamental garden plant. It has now taken over huge areas of land, and is in the top 100 worst invasive species in the Global Invasive Species Database (www.issg.org).

WORD BANK
ecosystem biological environment in which all the organisms in a particular place interact
pollinator something or someone tht carries pollen from one flower to another

Saving habitats

Governments around the world are setting aside important areas of land, both for the protection of the landscape and wildlife and for people to enjoy. There are national parks, wilderness areas, nature reserves, wildlife sanctuaries and refuges, game reserves, protected areas, and national monuments. Yellowstone National Park in the United States, created in 1872, was the world's first national park. There are now about 7,000 national parks and about 131,000 other protected areas all over the world.

The geysers and hot springs, together with buffalo, wolves, and grizzly bears, were the reasons why US President Ulysses S. Grant created Yellowstone National park in 1872.

Fragmentation

One problem with smaller nature reserves is that they become islands surrounded by unprotected areas, such as agricultural land. Animals, especially the larger **species**, cannot move about freely. They become isolated from their own kind, and their population cannot be increased. One answer to this problem is to create "wildlife corridors" between reserves. On the Indian sub-continent, an opportunity to do this came from an unexpected discovery.

Corridors for tigers

The tiger is one of the world's most **endangered** species. There are believed to be fewer than 3,200 tigers surviving in the wild. Many live in isolated jungle reserves. However, during a BBC wildlife filming expedition in 2010, tigers were discovered in the Himalayan foothills of Bhutan.

Now, the race is on for the Tiger Corridor Initiative. This is an organization that aims to create a 1,000 kilometre- (620 mile-) long "tiger corridor" that will link up surviving groups of tigers living in the foothills of the Himalayas – from Nepal into Bhutan, northern India, and Myanmar. Few people live in the mountains, so the tigers can roam undisturbed and safe from the threat of human activity in the towns, villages, and farms further south. It is a ray of hope for this critically endangered species.

Special unmanned camera traps set in Bhutan's mountains recorded tigers living high in the foothills, close to the edge of the tree line.

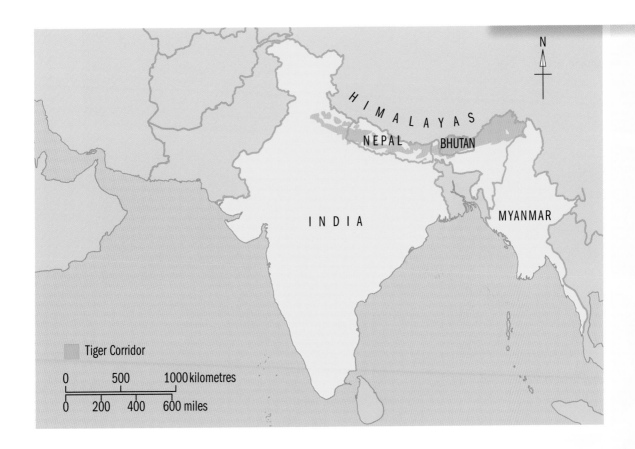

HIMALAYAS

NEPAL

BHUTAN

INDIA

MYANMAR

N

Tiger Corridor

| 0 | 500 | 1000 kilometres |

| 0 | 200 | 400 | 600 miles |

A crisis for frogs

Frogs and many other amphibians are in serious trouble. Thirty-two **species** of amphibians have become extinct in recent years. A further 200 species are believed to be under threat, especially frogs. The extinction of each species is directly linked with at least one of the threats to the future of wildlife that are discussed in this book. Frogs are an early warning of a world in deep trouble.

The Archey's frog of New Zealand is the world's most ancient species of frog. It is also top of the Zoological Society of London's Edge of Extinction list.

The trouble with muck

Frogs are victims of **habitat** destruction – and they are especially vulnerable to pollution. Frogs not only breathe through their skin; they can also absorb **toxic** chemicals through their skin. **Pesticides**, such as **DDT**, and industrial waste, such as **PCBs** (used by the electrical industry and in coolants), upset the frog's reproductive system so they are unable to produce offspring. Even some supposedly "safe" pesticides that are commonly used by gardeners are poisonous both to tadpoles and to adult frogs.

WHAT IT MEANS FOR US

Frogs are also being eaten to extinction – by humans. An estimated 180 million to 1 billion frogs worldwide are harvested each year. Frogs' legs are a popular meal in France, as well as in restaurants across Asia. In the past, French restaurant chefs collected frogs from the surrounding countryside. However, a decrease in local frog populations means that chefs are now importing frogs from other parts of the world, especially from southern and south-east Asia. For example, Indonesia exports over 5,000 tonnes of frog meat each year. Most of this goes to restaurants in Europe and the United States.

According to the UN Commodity Trade Statistics Database, the international trade in frogs' legs has increased during the past 20 years.

Alien invaders

Invasive alien species are also a threat to frog populations in many countries. For example, in Australia, native frogs and their tadpoles are **prey** for invader cane toads, crayfish, and rats. Tadpoles are also eaten by mosquito fish (plague minnow), a fish species that can survive in extreme conditions just about anywhere.

A change in the weather

Climate change and global warming are also having an effect on frog life. The timing of frog breeding cycles, for example, is influenced by temperature. Frogs' hibernation habits are also influenced by temperature. Due to global warming, frogs are emerging from their winter hibernation too early. Then they are caught out by sudden cold weather, and die. A rise in temperature might also suppress frogs' immune system, making them less able to fight disease.

Killer fungus

The most disturbing threat to frogs is disease. Frogs are dying from a serious water-borne fungal disease called chytridiomycosis, or chytrid. This has spread across the world, causing mass deaths of many frog species. However, scientists have discovered the way in which chytrid kills frogs.

The fungus attacks their moist skin, preventing important **elements**, such as sodium and potassium, from being absorbed by the body. These elements are important to a frog's well-being. For example, they help nerves to function properly. Without them, the frog's heart stops beating, and it dies.

Scientists in South America test a new species of stubfoot frog (discovered in 2007) for signs of the chytrid fungus.

Unravelling the genes

Some species of frogs are immune to the chytrid fungus, including African clawed frogs. In 2010, scientists announced that they had worked out the entire **genome** of one species of clawed frog. This is an important development for frog conservation.

Further research will identify the **genes** responsible for the clawed frog's immunity to the disease. This knowledge could be used in captive breeding programmes (see page 28). Scientists would be able to identify frogs from threatened species that are resistant to the disease and breed from those individuals. In this way, they would be sure their offspring survive. Eventually, they could be released back into the wild. The species would have a chance to recover.

Background extinctions

The extinction rate of amphibians today has been estimated to be 25,000–45,000 times the normal rate of extinction (known as background extinctions, because they are going on all the time in the background). It means that amphibians, such as the splendid leaf frog below, are disappearing from Earth unusually quickly.

Saving species

Cute and cuddly, the giant panda is instantly recognizable. In 1961, it became a symbol of the conservation movement as the logo of what was then the World Wildlife Fund (WWF). It was on the brink of extinction, but a programme of captive breeding in China has saved it, at least for the moment.

Captive breeding

One way to save **endangered** animals is to breed them in captivity in zoos, safari parks, and game farms. They can then be released back into the wild, but only if their natural **habitat** is still intact.

One of the first successful projects involved the Arabian oryx. By 1972, the oryx were hunted to extinction in the wild. However, in 1962, before they disappeared completely, the United Kingdom's Fauna and Flora Preservation Society took some oryx from the wild and bred a captive herd. They were sent to Phoenix Zoo, Arizona, in the United States. More breeding groups of oryx were established in other zoos around the world. Then, in 1982, the Arabian oryx were taken back to the wild.

Since that time, wild herds of oryx have been established in Oman, Saudi Arabia, and Israel. Similar captive breeding programmes have also been successful with Californian condors and black-footed ferrets in the United States, and golden lion tamarins in Brazil.

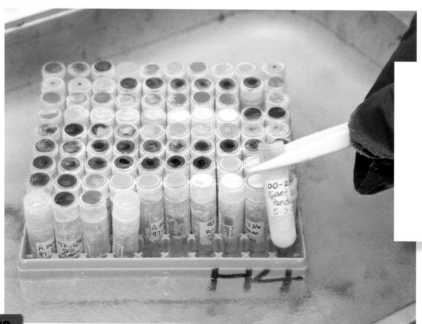

At the "Frozen Zoo" in San Diego, USA, tissues from over 800 species of endangered animals are frozen in liquid nitrogen and stored.

Preserving and breeding

Another way to ensure the future of threatened species is to store their seeds, embryos, sperm, and eggs, as well as tissue samples from which **DNA** can be extracted. Then, if the species becomes extinct in the wild, it can be brought back to life. Seeds can be planted and more seeds harvested until there are enough to replant in the wild. Animal embryos can be implanted into **surrogate** mothers, probably females from a closely related species. When sufficient numbers have been bred, they can be returned to the wild.

Questions to think about

Can you name five plants that you relied on today? What have you eaten? What are you wearing? How different would your life be if those plants were extinct?

The Millennium Seed Bank at Kew Gardens has the seeds of 24,200 plant species in storage.

What can I do?

Can small-scale actions have any impact on large-scale problems?

Everybody in the world has a "carbon footprint". This is the amount of **greenhouse gas** emissions, such as carbon dioxide (CO_2), caused by our activities. If we buy vegetables grown locally, our carbon footprint is lower than if we buy vegetables shipped in from overseas. This is because the amount of CO_2 released by the burning fuel of a lorry carrying our vegetables from the local farm is much less than if they are transported by a ship or aircraft across the world.

Actions, not words

One thing we can all do is to look at the way we live and see if we can make changes that will lower our carbon footprint. These may only be small changes, but if everyone tried to lower their footprint it could have a significant effect on global warming. (See the "Topics to research" section on page 47 for a way to measure your carbon footprint.)

Here are a number of simple things you and your family can do to reduce your carbon footprint:

- Reduce waste by choosing reusable products rather than disposable ones.
- Buy products with the least packaging (for example, loose vegetables rather than packaged ones).
- Recycle paper, plastic, newspaper, glass, and aluminium cans.
- Insulate walls and attics; put weather stripping around doors and windows or install double-glazing.
- Replace standard light bulbs with low-energy ones (compact fluorescent light bulbs).
- Walk and cycle instead of going by car; walk to the local shops instead of driving to the supermarket.
- Turn off lights when leaving a room; turn off TVs and computers when they are not in use.
- Use less hot water.
- Turn off the water when brushing your teeth.
- Set the thermostat for the central heating a couple of degrees lower than usual.

Cycling is healthy as well as low on CO_2 emissions. Only your breath gives off CO_2 when you cycle.

One person can make a difference. When CO_2 savings for one person's well-insulated home are scaled up to the population of a town or a country, we can change the world.

Something to think about

If every home in the United Kingdom installed at least three low-energy light bulbs, enough energy would be saved to power the whole country's street lighting.

The CO_2 savings for...	...would be
One person	900 kilograms (2,000 pounds)
A small country e.g. Belgium	9.4 billion kilograms (20.8 billion pounds)
A medium country e.g. Thailand	58.6 billion kilograms (129.2 billion pounds)
A large country e.g. United States	270.7 billion kilograms (596.8 billion pounds), which is about the same as half the total annual CO_2 emissions in the United Kingdom.

Clues from the past

We've looked at what is happening to life on Earth right now, but to really understand its prospects in the future, we need to look at what happened in the past. Global warming occurred naturally millions of years ago, but human activity is causing the global warming that is happening today.

High CO_2

The last time carbon dioxide (CO_2) levels were high was 15 to 20 million years ago. With sustained high levels of CO_2, the global temperature was 3–6 degrees Celsius (5–10 degrees Fahrenheit) higher than it is today. The sea level rose 23–37 metres (75–120 feet). CO_2 levels rose to 400 parts per million. There was no permanent ice in the Arctic, and the Greenland and Antarctic ice sheets were much smaller. In other words, the planet was different from how it is today. North and South America were separated by sea, and the largest **predatory** shark that ever lived (*Megalodon*) patrolled the warm oceans.

This photo shows the fossilized jaw of a *Megalodon*. It grew to 20 metres (67 feet) long and lived between 1.5 and 25 million years ago, when it fed on whales and dolphins in warm ocean waters.

History repeats itself

For almost 800,000 years, CO_2 levels have changed very little. There has been between 180 and 300 parts per million of CO_2 in the atmosphere. But widespread burning of fossils fuels, starting with the **Industrial Revolution**, has led to the dramatic rise in the CO_2 level to the 374 parts per million we see today. We are rapidly approaching the 400 parts per million which existed 15 to 20 million years ago. Some scientists forecast even higher levels – to 600 or even 900 parts per million during the next century. What effect do you think this is likely to have on the world we live in?

The chart shows CO_2 levels in parts per million (ppm) in the past, with several different projections into the future made by the **Intergovernmental Panel on Climate Change (IPCC)**.

Common confusions

Natural or unnatural?
Some people say that global warming is due to natural events. However, it is unlikely that the rapid warming of Earth's climate that we see today is caused by natural cycles. Temperature increases in the past took place over a far greater length of time. Also, computer models of Earth's climate cannot reproduce the climate changes we are seeing today without including emissions of CO_2 caused by human activity.

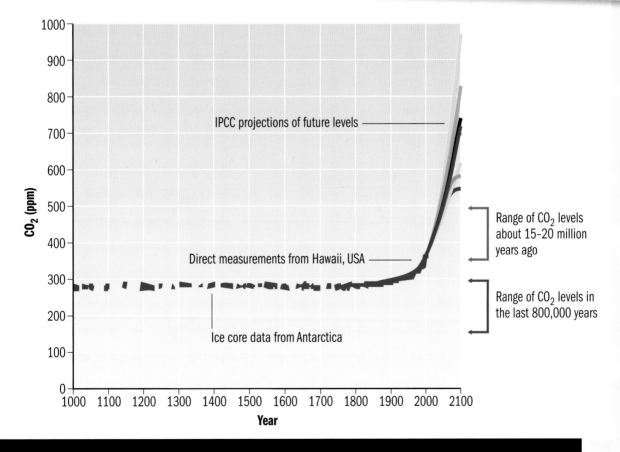

IPCC projections of future levels

Direct measurements from Hawaii, USA

Ice core data from Antarctica

Range of CO_2 levels about 15–20 million years ago

Range of CO_2 levels in the last 800,000 years

CO_2 (ppm)

Year

WORD BANK

Intergovernmental Panel on Climate Change (IPCC) organization that studies information from around

Mass extinctions: who's next?

When we look into the past, we find there have been times when life was almost wiped off the face of the planet. There have been many of these "mass extinctions" in Earth's history, but there were at least five big ones. They had an enormous influence on how life **evolved** and its very future on Earth.

The "Big Five" mass extinction events

Extinction event	Millions of years ago	Impact
Ordovician-Silurian	443.7	Second largest event; took place over 3 million years with 85% of ocean **species** becoming extinct, including trilobites. (Trilobites are invertebrates with hard **exoskeletons** and segmented legs, slightly similar to modern horseshoe crabs.)
Late Devonian	359.2	A series of extinctions over 3 million years, with a loss of 70% of mostly ocean species, including jawless fish, primitive armour-clad fishes that probably fed by sucking food into the mouth.
Permian-Triassic	251.0	World's largest extinction event, when 90–95% of ocean species and 70% of land species were eliminated.
Triassic-Jurassic	199.6	In less than 10,000 years, 50% of known species became extinct, including large amphibians, paving the way for the dinosaurs.
Cretaceous-Tertiary	65.95	About 50% of known species disappeared, including dinosaurs, mosasaurs, plesiosaurs, and pterosaurs. The birds (which evolved from the dinosaurs) and mammals survived.

Outer space or inner Earth?

It is very difficult to identify what actually caused these mass extinctions. There are many theories. One explanation put forward for the extinction of the dinosaurs is that it was caused by a comet or asteroid ploughing into Earth. Around the world, asteriods have left impact craters that coincide in age with extinction events. On Mexico's Yucatán Peninsula, the Chicxulub impact crater is thought to be the result of a piece of asteroid slamming into our planet just before the dinosaur extinctions 65.95 million years ago.

Sixth great mass extinction

Scientists believe we are entering, or are already in the midst of, the sixth mass extinction. This extinction event is caused not by asteroids or volcanoes but is partly down to us. Global warming, **habitat** destruction, and all the other damage that humans have caused to the **environment** are causing more and more more species to disappear. The International Union for Conservation of Nature is an organization that works to find solutions to environment and development challenges. By 2008, it had assessed 44,837 species. At least 12,038 of these have been classified as threatened and 804 classified as extinct. For this reason, scientists feel the sixth great mass extinction is well under way.

A popular theory is that hunting and competition for land by humans caused the extinction of the woolly mammoth. However, studies have concluded that it died out because climate change caused a massive decline in its grassland habitat.

Massive eruptions

At about the same time as the asteroid hit Earth, immense volcanic eruptions occurred in central India (60–68 million years ago). They lasted on and off for thousands of years, spewing lava over half of India. Some scientists believe that the dust and **aerosols** flung into the atmosphere by these eruptions contributed to the dinosaurs' disappearance. Whatever the cause, not all plants and animals were wiped out. Freshwater species such as crocodiles and frogs survived, as did birds and small mammals.

Near miss

So, could such a major catastrophe occur again? It is certainly possible that we could be hit by a large asteroid or comet in the future. Scientists have identified over 7,000 "Near Earth Objects" – asteroids whose orbits have come very close to Earth.

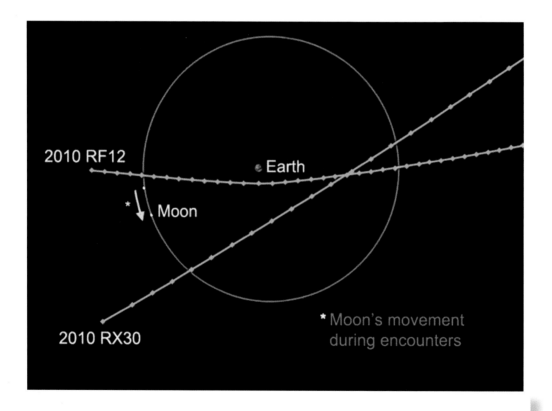

Two Near Earth Objects came close to Earth on 8 September 2010. The first, called 2010 RX30, flew past at a distance of 248,000 kilometres (154,000 miles). The second, 2010 RF12, came to within 79,000 kilometres (49,000 miles) of our planet, inside the Moon's orbit. It was the first time two asteroids had been seen close to Earth in quick succession.

Objects smaller than about 25 metres (80 feet) across burn up in the atmosphere before they hit Earth – but there are bigger objects coming close, too. In 2029, for example, an asteroid about 270 metres (890 feet) across, known as 99942 Apophis, is expected to pass close to Earth. It will be the first of three close encounters by Apophis. It is stark reminder that our planet is vulnerable and the future of life on Earth is far from certain, even without the threats posed by human activity.

The Apophis asteroid is scheduled to pass close to Earth in 2029 and 2036.

Brave new world

Whilst many plant and animal **species** were eliminated during the great mass extinction events of the past, other species did well. This was mostly due to sheer luck. They were in the right place at the right time. They may not have been superior species, but they could flourish because there was no longer any competition from other, more dominant species.

Weighing in at 15–20 tonnes, *Paraceratherium* was the largest terrestrial mammal ever to have lived. It was a prehistoric relative of the rhinoceros, but browsed on trees like a giraffe. It lived about 23–34 million years ago and became extinct when its forests disappeared and dry prairies took their place.

Accelerated evolution

After the disappearance of the dinosaurs 65.95 million years ago, the birds and mammals took over. The mammals had been small, insignificant creatures. However, as soon as the dinosaurs were gone, mammals emerged from the shadows. It was their turn to dominate the planet. Some mammals grew to rival the giant dinosaurs in size.

Who takes over?

In the future, which species do you think might take over from those being wiped out by humans? For clues, we can look at what is going on in the oceans. The likely candidates may come as a surprise.

The oceans are suffering from **habitat** destruction, overfishing, invasive alien species, pollution, and the massive runoff of fertilizers from the land into rivers and then into the sea. The once rich and complex marine **ecosystems**, such as coral reefs and kelp forests, are being turned into a flat and monotonous seabed. Coastal seas are becoming **anoxic** dead zones – that is, areas where the water contains no oxygen. Here, disease-causing **micro-organisms**, **toxic dinoflagellate** blooms, and jellyfish dominate the sea. For example, conditions in some parts of the ocean favour jellyfish rather than fish. Overfishing removes jellyfish **predators**, so jellyfish populations soar.

Jellyfish have become an ongoing problem in the Mediterranean where the painful mauve stinger terrorizes holidaymakers. Swarms of jellyfish can be so big and bulky that they sink fishing nets and clog up the water intakes of power stations. In 2007, an enormous 26-square-kilometre (10-square-mile) swarm of mauve stingers killed all 100,000 fish on a salmon farm in Northern Ireland. If this is a sample of what is happening in the oceans right now, the future for the diversity of life looks bleak.

The mauve stinger is just one of an army of jellyfish that is beginning to take over the seas.

WORD BANK
anoxic   devoid of oxygen
dinoflagellate   one of a group of plankton that are poisonous to ocean animals

Armageddon

Does life on Earth have a long-term future?

Ultimately, the future for life on Earth depends on the Sun, 149 million kilometres (93 million miles) away. The Sun's energy supports almost all life on Earth by **photosynthesis** (an exception being **organisms** that live at hydrothermal vents on the ocean floor). It also drives the climate and weather on our planet. However, one day the Sun will change. It is currently about halfway through its 10 billion-year life as a main star. In 5 billion years' time, it will expand into a red giant, with its outer layers engulfing Earth.

The end of life as we know it

According to one theory, as the Sun brightens, the climate on Earth will get hotter, with more rain falling. The rain will weather more rock. This will dissolve carbon dioxide (CO_2) and store it away as calcium carbonate (the same material that makes corals and seashells) on the ocean floor.

Eventually, the level of CO_2 in the atmosphere would be so low that there would not be enough for plants to photosynthesize. This would destroy the foundation of most food chains on the planet. Then, the oceans would evaporate entirely and the water vapour drift off into space. Earth would become an arid desert, like Mars. In little over a billion years, life as we know it would cease, except perhaps for a few extremophiles (see page 11). This would be well before it would have become a red giant.

If calculations by geophysicist Professor James Kasting of Pennsylvania State University are correct, Earth's surface could be like that of Mars in less than a billion years.

Future ark?

So, what will happen to humans? By the time the Sun reaches its dangerous period, we could be long gone from Earth. It is possible that people in the future will travel outside our solar system to search for stars like our Sun and planets like our Earth. If people took samples of life on Earth with them, there could be a long-term future for life on a "new" Earth. But they would need to choose which plants and animals to take, and which to leave behind. Which organisms would you take?

At home on Titan?

The conditions on Saturn's largest moon Titan (below) are similar to Earth when life **evolved** here. Jupiter's moon Europa has oxygen and water ice. Both are possible staging posts for Earth-life colonies when the Sun expands. Perhaps we will be headed for the Gliese 581 solar system, 20.3 light years away, with its newly discovered Earth-like planets.

Earth's threatened species

Decline of marine life from before human exploitation to the present day

Bull sharks off North Carolina, USA	99%	Oceanic whitetip sharks in the Gulf of Mexico	99%
Coastal eagles and other raptors	79%	Oysters	91%
Cod in north-west Atlantic	96%	Scalloped hammerhead sharks off North Carolina, USA	98%
Commercial sponges off the coast of Florida, USA	89%	Sea grass	65%
Fish weighing 4–66 kg (9–145 lbs.) in the North Sea	97–99%	Sea turtles	87%
Great white sharks in north-west Atlantic	79%	Seabirds	57%
Green turtles in the Caribbean	99%	Seals and otters	55%
Hammerhead sharks in north-west Atlantic	89%	Shorebirds	61%
Hawksbill turtles in the Caribbean	99%	Silky sharks in the Gulf of Mexico	91%
Large **predatory** fish e.g. tuna	90%	Small whales	59%
Large whales	85%	Thresher sharks in north-west Atlantic	80%
Live coral cover in the Caribbean	80–93%	Tiger sharks off North Carolina	97%
Manatees and sea cows	90%		
Mussels	47%		

Unless specified location is given, the decline is global.

Estimated number of species and threatened species on Earth

Group	Known species	Threatened species in 1996–1998	Threatened species in 2010
VERTEBRATES			
Mammals (excluding domestic animals)	5,491	1,096	1,131
Birds	10,027	1,107	1,240
Reptiles	9,205	253	594
Amphibians	6,638	124	1,898
Fishes	31,800	734	1,851
INVERTEBRATES			
Insects	1,000,000	537	733
Molluscs	85,000	920	1,288
Crustaceans	47,000	407	596
Corals	2,175	1	235
Arachnids	102,248	11	19
Velvet worms	165	6	9
Horseshoe crabs	4	0	0
Others	68,658	9	24
PLANTS AND PLANT-LIKE ORGANISMS			
Mosses, hornworts, and liverworts	16,236	-	80
Ferns, club mosses, spike mosses, and quillworts	12,000	-	148
Gymnosperms	1,052	142	371
Flowering plants	268,000	-	8,116
Green algae	4,242	-	0
Red algae	6,144	-	9
FUNGI AND PROTISTS			
Lichens	17,000	-	2
Mushrooms	31,496	-	1
Brown algae	3,127	-	6

Glossary

adapt become better suited to the environment

aerosol fine liquid or solid particles suspended in gas

annelid worm one of the segmented worms, which includes the earthworm

anoxic devoid of oxygen

bacterium (plural: **bacteria**) single-celled micro-organism with no distinct nucleus. Bacteria are the most abundant life forms on Earth.

biodiversity variety of life in the world or in a particular habitat

climate change long-term change in weather patterns

concentrate make denser, stronger, or purer

contaminate pollute or make dirty

DDT long-acting pesticide used on crops to kill pest insects

desalination process to remove salt from sea water to make fresh water

dinoflagellate one of a group of plankton that are poisonous to ocean animals. In turn, these are poisonous to humans who eat them.

DNA contains the genetic instruction of an organism

dormant inactive

echolocation way of finding objects by bouncing sounds off them

ecosystem biological environment in which all the organisms living in a particular place interact

element pure chemical substance

endangered at risk of disappearing forever

environment living and non-living surroundings of an individual

evolve develop by the process of gradual change from one generation to the next

exoskeleton external supportive covering

gene basic unit of inheritance

genetically modified has had its genetic make-up altered artificially

genome total hereditary information of an organism

greenhouse gas gas that absorbs the Sun's energy and radiates it back into the atmosphere, causing the greenhouse effect

groundwater water located below the land surface in soil or cracks in rocks

habitat environment in which a species or organism lives

hectare measurement of area of about 10,000 square metres (2.5 acres)

Industrial Revolution major changes in industry, agriculture, mining, and transport that began during the 1800s

Intergovernmental Panel on Climate Change (IPCC) organization that studies information from around the world concerning climate change

life expectancy how long a person is expected to live

micro-organism living thing that cannot be seen with the naked eye

organism any kind of living thing

outback desert-like interior of Australia

parasite organism that lives on or in other organisms and causes harm to the host

PCB chemical pollutant once used in many different industries (now banned)

photosynthesis process that plants use to make food using light energy from the Sun

pollinator something or someone that carries pollen from one flower to another

predator animal or plant that catches and eats animals

prey animal caught and eaten by other animals or plants

pesticide substance used on crops or in gardens to destroy or repel pests

radiation something given out by radioactive substances

rain-seeding creating clouds and rain artificially

saltpan dry, flat plain of salt

species basic category of biological classification, composed of related individuals that are able to breed amongst themselves but not with other species

stratosphere second major layer in Earth's atmosphere, above the troposphere (lowest layer)

surrogate substitute; one who takes the place of another

temperate climatic region of Earth between the tropics and the poles

toxic poisonous

ultraviolet part of sunlight that is invisible to humans. Ultraviolet rays cause sunburn.

vacuum volume of space that is empty of matter, such that its gas pressure is less than atmospheric pressure

Find out more

Books

Climate: The Force that Shapes Our World and the Future of Life on Earth, George Ochoa, Jennifer Hoffman, and Tina Tin (Rodale Books, 2005)

Planet Earth: As You've Never Seen It Before, Alastair Fothergill (with a forward by David Attenborough), (BBC Books, 2006)

Planet Earth, The Future: What the Experts Say, Rosamund Kidman Cox and Fergus Beeley (eds), (BBC Books, 2006)

The Blue Planet: A Natural History of the Oceans, Andrew Byatt, Alastair Fothergill, and Martha Holmes (with a forward by David Attenborough), (BBC Books, 2001)

DVDs/Blue-ray

Planet Earth (2006), BBC Natural History Unit series, which takes a definitive look at the diversity of life on our planet. Narrated by David Attenborough. (*Planet Earth, The Future* is included on DVD sets but is absent from HD DVD and Blue-ray editions), BBCDVD1883

Blue Planet (2001), BBC Natural History Unit series, which takes a definitive, look at the diversity of life in the sea. Narrated by David Attenborough. Four-disc special edition (UK), BBCDVD1792

The Future is Wild (2004), a natural history of the future including animation and expert comment, Paramount Home Entertainment, UK 111126

Websites

www.jpl.nasa.gov
Jet Propulsion Laboratory of California Institute of Technology, including:
Asteroid Watch at: **www.jpl.nasa.gov/asteroidwatch**
Global Climate Change at: **climate.nasa.gov**
Exoplanet Exploration at: **planetquest.jpl.nasa.gov**

www.arkive.org
Arkive from Wildscreen with information, stills, and video images from the world's leading wildlife photographers and filmmakers about the world's endangered species

www.iucnredlist.org
IUCN Red List of threatened species and their status as listed by the World Conservation Union

www.panda.org
World Wide Fund for Nature (International)

www.wwf.org.uk
World Wide Fund for Nature (UK)

www.fauna-flora.org
Fauna and Flora International, formerly the Flora and Fauna Preservation Society of the UK, which has been saving endangered species and habitats around the world since its founding in 1903

www.conservation.org
Conservation International, focusing on healthy ecosystems and human well-being since 1987

www.nationalgeographic.com
National Geographic Society

www.birdlife.org
BirdLife International, working together for birds and people

www.plantlife.org.uk
Plantlife, focusing on the wild plants of the British Isles

www.nature.org
The Nature Conservancy, protecting Earth's most important natural places

www.wetlands.org
Wetlands International, working to sustain and restore wetlands and their resources for people and biodiversity since 1954

www.kew.org
Royal Botanic Gardens. Find out about the Kew and Millennium Seed Bank.

www.sandiegozoo.org/conservation/science/at_the_zoo/the_frozen_zoo
Frozen Zoo and San Diego Zoo conservation projects

Topics to research

Web pages for more than 80,000 marine species described by the Census of Marine Life (COML) scientists can be found in the Encyclopedia of Life at: www.eol.org.

Find out more about the work of The Blacksmith Institute, a non-profit organization based in New York City, USA, that helps clean up pollution and save lives around the world.

You can research the everyday energy use of you and your family, then calculate your carbon footprints by logging on to: calc.zerofootprint.net/youth or www.planet-positive.org/how_2_kidscalc.php

Index